Life Among the Olmecs

Daily Life of the Native American People
Olmec (1200-400 BC)

Social Studies 5th Grade | Children's Geography & Cultures Books

First Edition, 2020

Published in the United States by Speedy Publishing LLC, 40 E Main Street, Newark, Delaware 19711 USA.

© 2020 Baby Professor Books, an imprint of Speedy Publishing LLC

All rights reserved.

Without limiting the rights under the copyright reserved above, no part of this publication may be reproduced, stored in or introduced into a retrieval system, or transmitted, in any form, or by any means (electronic, mechanical, photocopying, recording, or otherwise), without the prior written permission of the copyright owner.

All images in this book have been reproduced with the knowledge and prior consent of the artists concerned, and no responsibility is accepted by producer, publisher, or printer for any infringement of copyright or otherwise arising from the contents of this publication.

Baby Professor Books are available at special discounts when purchased in bulk for industrial and sales-promotional use. For details contact our Special Sales Team at Speedy Publishing LLC, 40 E Main Street, Newark, Delaware 19711 USA. Telephone (888) 248-4521 Fax: (210) 519-4043.

10 9 8 7 6 * 5 4 3 2 1

Print Edition: 9781541949973
Digital Edition: 9781541951778

See the world in pictures. Build your knowledge in style.
www.speedypublishing.com

Table of Contents

Who Were the Olmec People? 5
When Did the Olmec Civilization Begin and End? 15
Did the Olmec People Have a Writing System? 19
Olmec Trading and How It Influenced Daily Life 25
Hallmarks of the Olmec Civilization 35
Olmec Religious Beliefs 43
Olmec Expressions of Art 55
The Colossal Carved Heads 61
The End of the Olmec Civilization 67
Summary 71

In this book, we're going to talk about the Olmec civilization, so let's get right to it!

Who Were the Olmec People?

The Olmec were the first people to create a civilization in the region of North America we call Mexico today. Their complex society was the earliest civilization in Mesoamerica, which means "Middle America." If you were traveling in Mesoamerica, you would begin in the central section of Mexico and travel in a southeastern direction through numerous countries until you arrived in Costa Rica. The Olmec people lived in the lowland, coastal section of Mexico next to the Gulf of Mexico.

MAP OF THE OLMEC HEARTLAND, WHERE THE OLMEC REIGNED FROM 1400 TO 400 BCE

THE OLMEC RUINS BUILT WITH KILN-FIRED BRICKS IN TABASCO STATE, MEXICO

The Tuxtla Mountains cover the area. Today, this land is divided into two states of Mexico, Tabasco and Veracruz.

The word "Olmec" is derived not from their language, but from the Aztec civilization, which came after theirs. Translated from the language of Nahuatl, the word means "the people who work with rubber."

THE WORD OLMEC TRANSLATES TO "THE PEOPLE WHO WORK WITH RUBBER."

A CENTURIES-OLD LATEX BALL MADE BY THE OLMEC.

Archaeologists speculate that they were possibly the first civilization to figure out how to convert the raw latex from rubber trees into a substance that could be molded and used for many different purposes. Not only were they the first to make it, they also traded rubber extensively throughout the region.

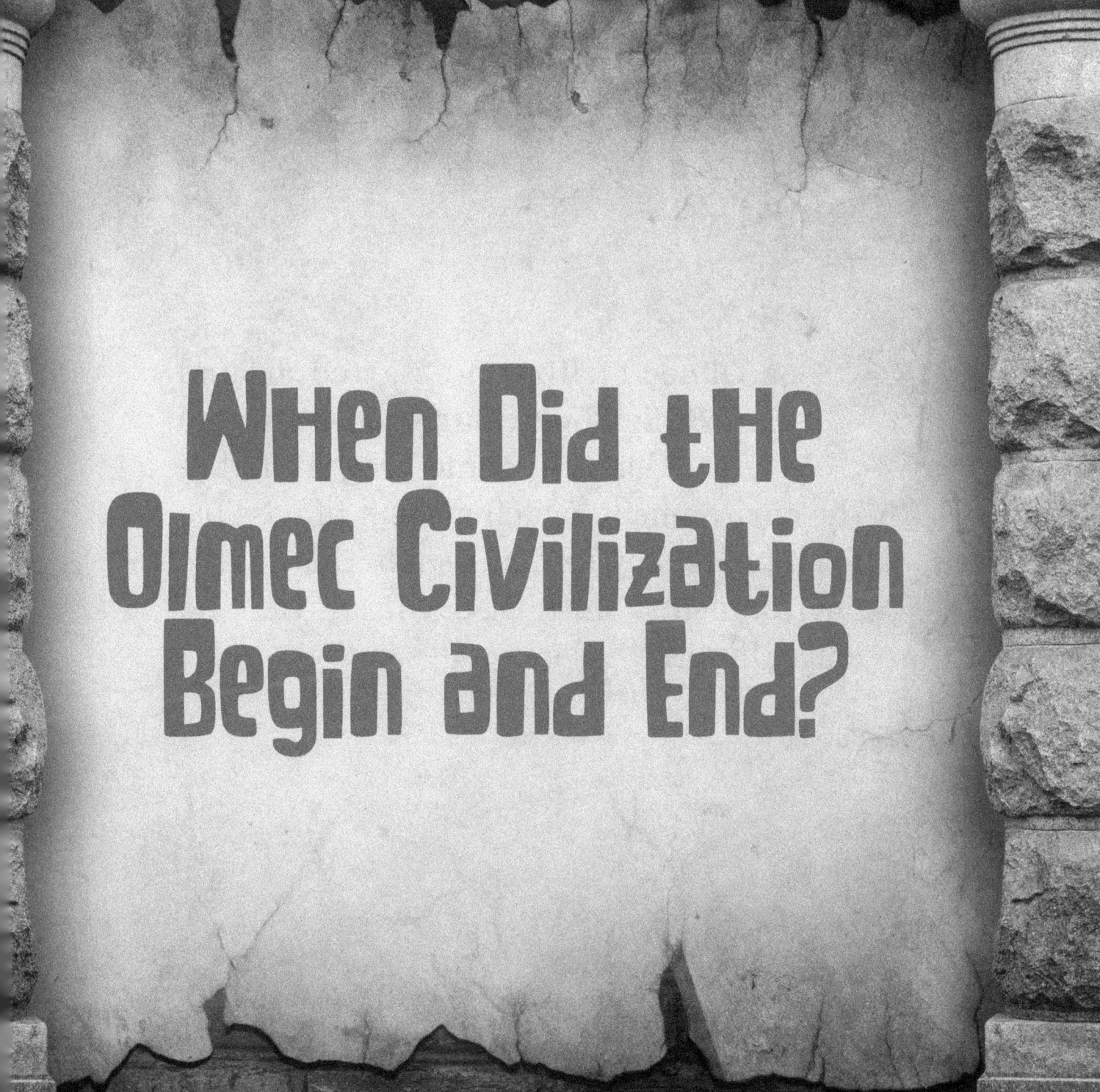

The Olmec civilization started around 1600 BCE. They flourished until 350 BCE. At that time something shifted in the environment, which made it impossible for them to stay in that region. Due to this environmental shift, their villages were no longer livable.

A DIORAMA OF THE MESOAMERICAN OLMEC CULTURES ON DISPLAY AT THE MUSEUM OF ANTHROPOLOGY IN THE HISTORIC CENTER OF XALAPA, VERACRUZ, MEXICO.

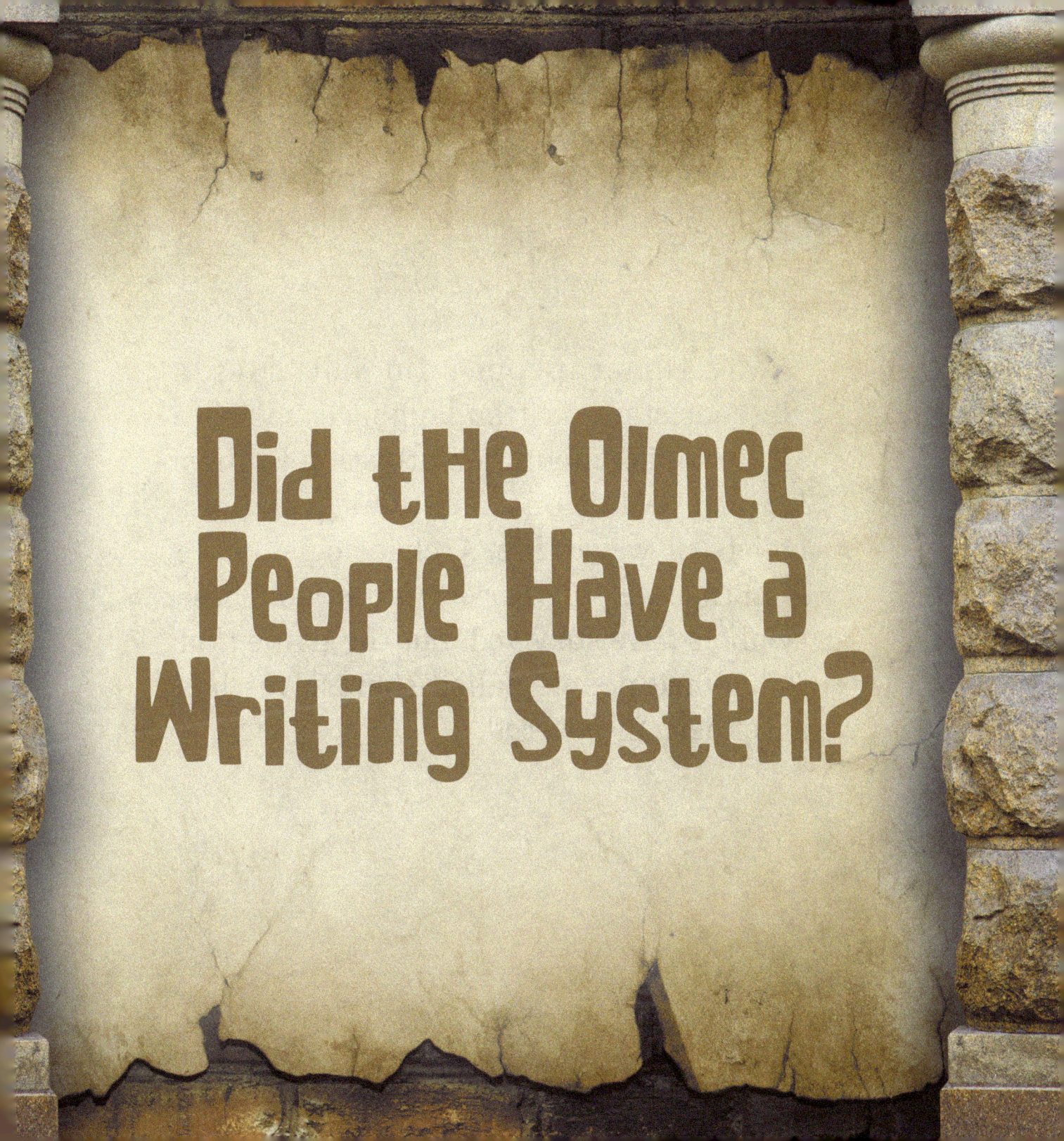

The Olmec people did not have a consistent written language, so there isn't documentation attesting to their history, traditions, customs, religious beliefs, or way of life. Archaeologists have found a few glyphs carved into stone. These symbols have survived, but the name that the Olmec people called themselves has never been discovered.

AN EXAMPLE OF OLMEC GLYPHS.

RESEARCHERS HAVE DETERMINED THAT THE OLMEC PEOPLE TRADED OVER A VAST REGION.

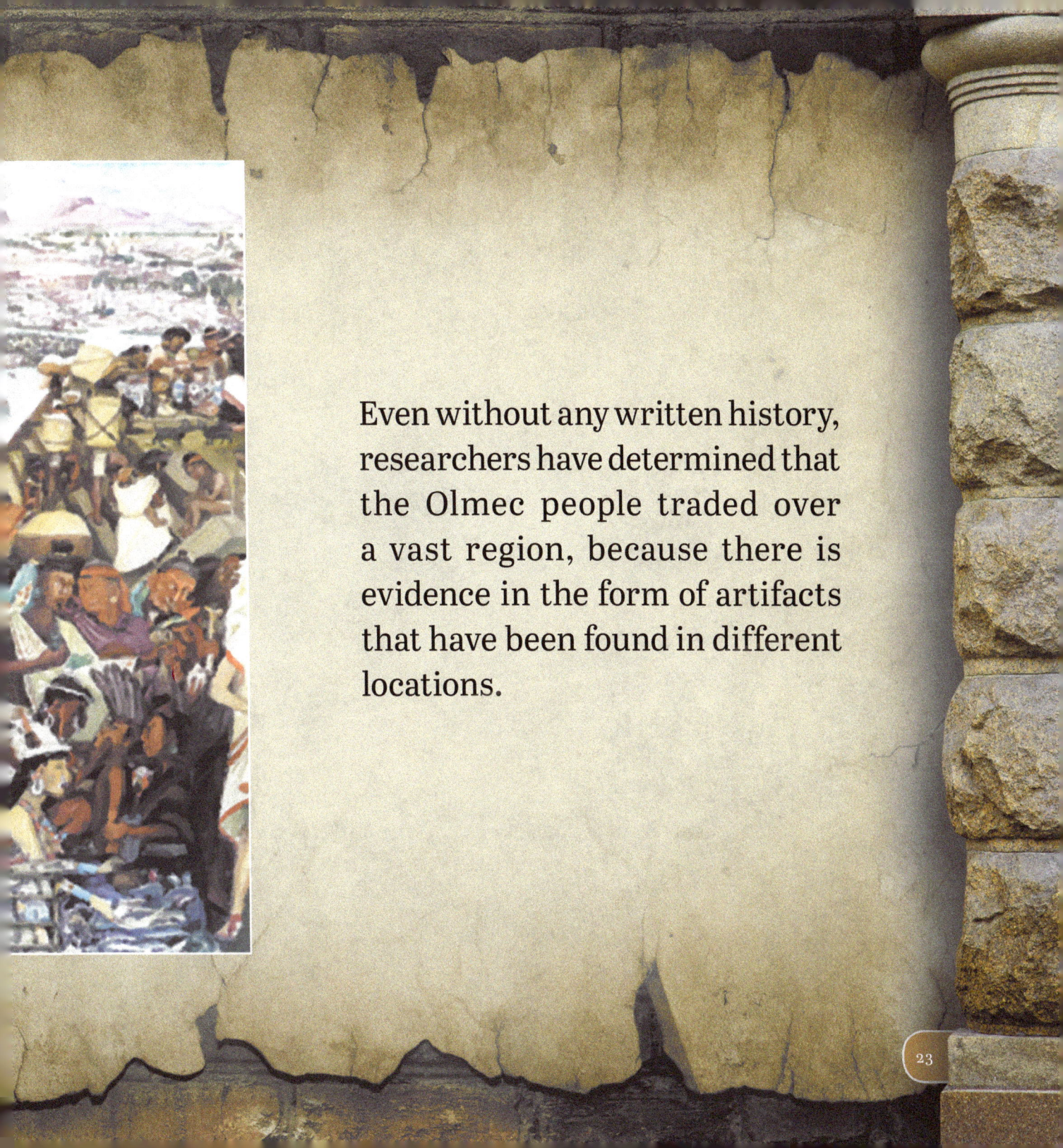

Even without any written history, researchers have determined that the Olmec people traded over a vast region, because there is evidence in the form of artifacts that have been found in different locations.

Olmec Trading and How It Influenced Daily Life

OBSIDIAN OLMEC NECKLACE

Researchers have unearthed artifacts created from jade, a type of green gemstone, as well as a volcanic, black, glossy rock called obsidian. Since the jade came from a faraway region of Mexico, called Oaxaca today, and the obsidian came from the region known as Guatemala today, they know that the Olmec people traded for these precious materials. To get these materials, they traded rubber. As the centuries passed, the Olmec civilization continued to add trade routes throughout Mesoamerica.

JADE OLMEC FIGURINES

Their success at trading helped them to create urban areas such as San Lorenzo and the city of La Venta. However, these areas were used for religious ceremonies and for activities that the leaders were engaged in, not for the common people.

OLMEC STONE ALTAR IN THE LA VENTA ARCHEOLOGICAL PARK IN VILLAHERMOSA, MEXICO

SAN LORENZO WAS A MAJOR CENTER OF OLMEC CULTURE.

THE OLMEC LIVED IN SMALLER VILLAGES.

The regular citizens lived in much smaller villages. Each dwelling included a structure that was similar to our modern sheds. They also had pits where they stored vegetables close to their homes. There's evidence that they had gardens. They grew herbs used for medicine as well as smaller crops, such as sunflowers.

Outside the village region, they cleared large fields using slashing and burning techniques. They grew many types of crops. They planted and harvested maize, which is corn, different types of beans and squash, manioc, which is a type of root vegetable, and sweet potatoes. They also planted cotton to create fabric.

THE OLMEC PLANTED AND HARVESTED MAIZE.

Hallmarks of the Olmec Civilization

The Olmec people are known today because of several key aspects of their culture. They are known for their incredible stone sculptures made of basalt, a type of rock formed from volcanic lava. These boulders were excavated from quarries and then carved in detail to represent their important leaders. Some of these sculptures weigh over 20 tons!

OLMEC BIG BASALT HEAD

A second important archaeological discovery was that the Olmec were more than likely the original creators of the popular Mesoamerican game that was played using solid balls of rubber. It's simply called the "ball game."

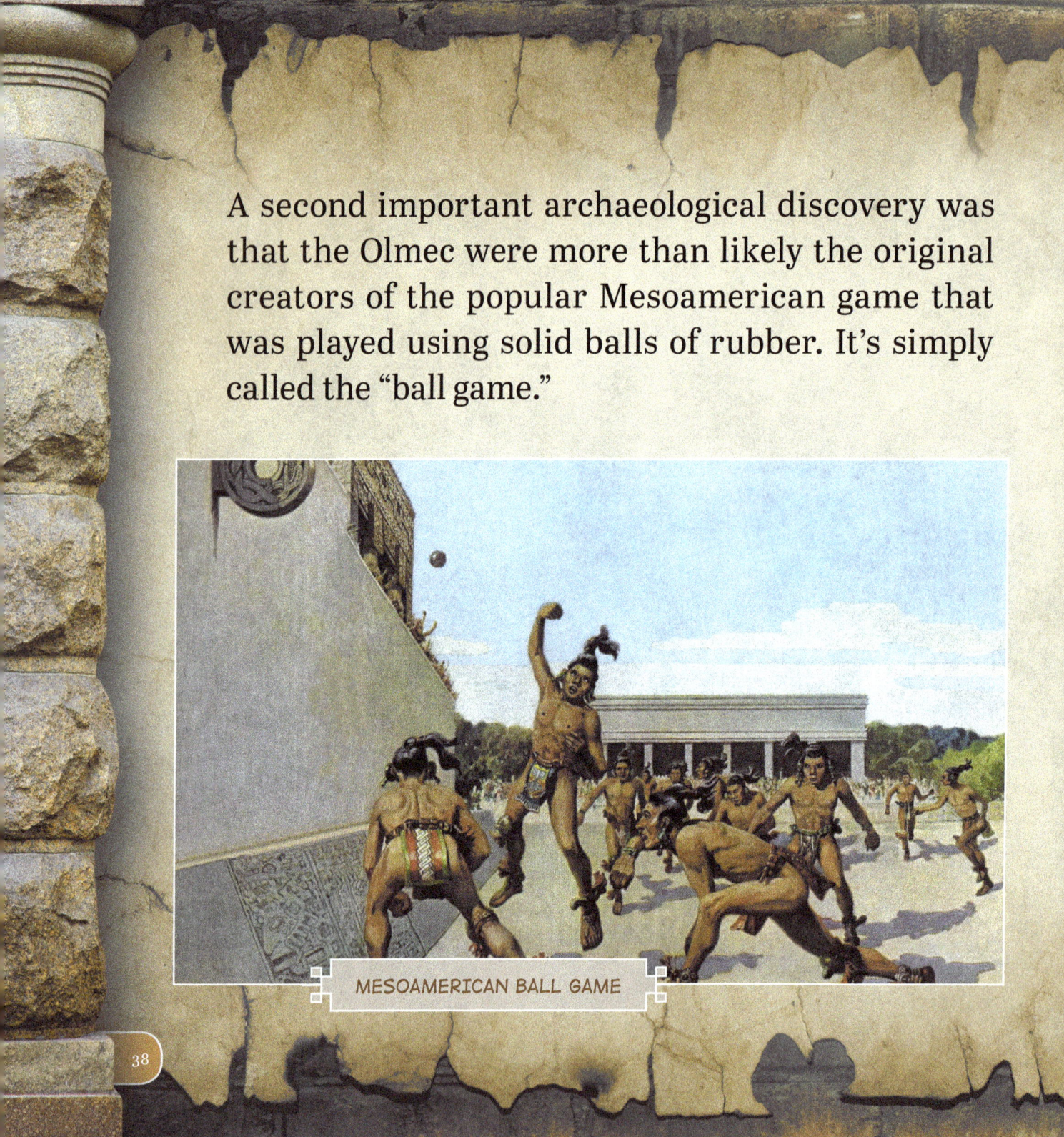
MESOAMERICAN BALL GAME

This wasn't just a sport however. It had religious significance. Sometimes the captain of the losing team or maybe the entire losing team was sacrificed up to the Olmec gods.

STONE CARVING FROM MAIN BALL COURT AT EL TAJIN, VERACRUZ, MEXICO SHOWING A HUMAN HEART SACRIFICE.

A third aspect of their culture was that they practiced bloodletting. They would pierce parts of their bodies with sharp implements as part of a religious ritual. The blood would spill onto a lump of incense or a piece of fabric or paper made of bark. Then, the blood-soaked item would be burned as part of a sacrifice to the sky gods.

A STONE CARVING DEPICTING THE OLMEC BLOODLETTING RITUAL – PASSING A SPIKED ROPE THROUGH THE TONGUE.

Olmec Religious Beliefs

Although there are no written records of the Olmec's religious beliefs, their amazing artwork provides clues about their religion as well as their rituals. Many of their pieces of art were carved in stone and have lasted for thousands of years.

OLMEC ROCK CARVING SCULPTURE AT OLMEC ARCHAEOLOGICAL MUSEUM, LA VENTA PARK IN VILLAHERMOSA, TABASCO, MEXICO

They were interested in the balance between male and female and this is shown in the eight different deities they carved. These carvings had both masculine and feminine features. In other words, their deities were depicted as androgynous.

OLMEC DIOS VIEJO STATUE FROM THE STATE OF VERACRUZ, NATIONAL MUSEUM OF ANTHROPOLOGY, CHAPULTEPEC PARK, MEXICO CITY

The gods that they represented in stone were often associated with a natural force or a type of animal. For example, one of their deities, the Bird Monster, was depicted as a harpy eagle, which represented leadership and the qualities of a powerful ruler.

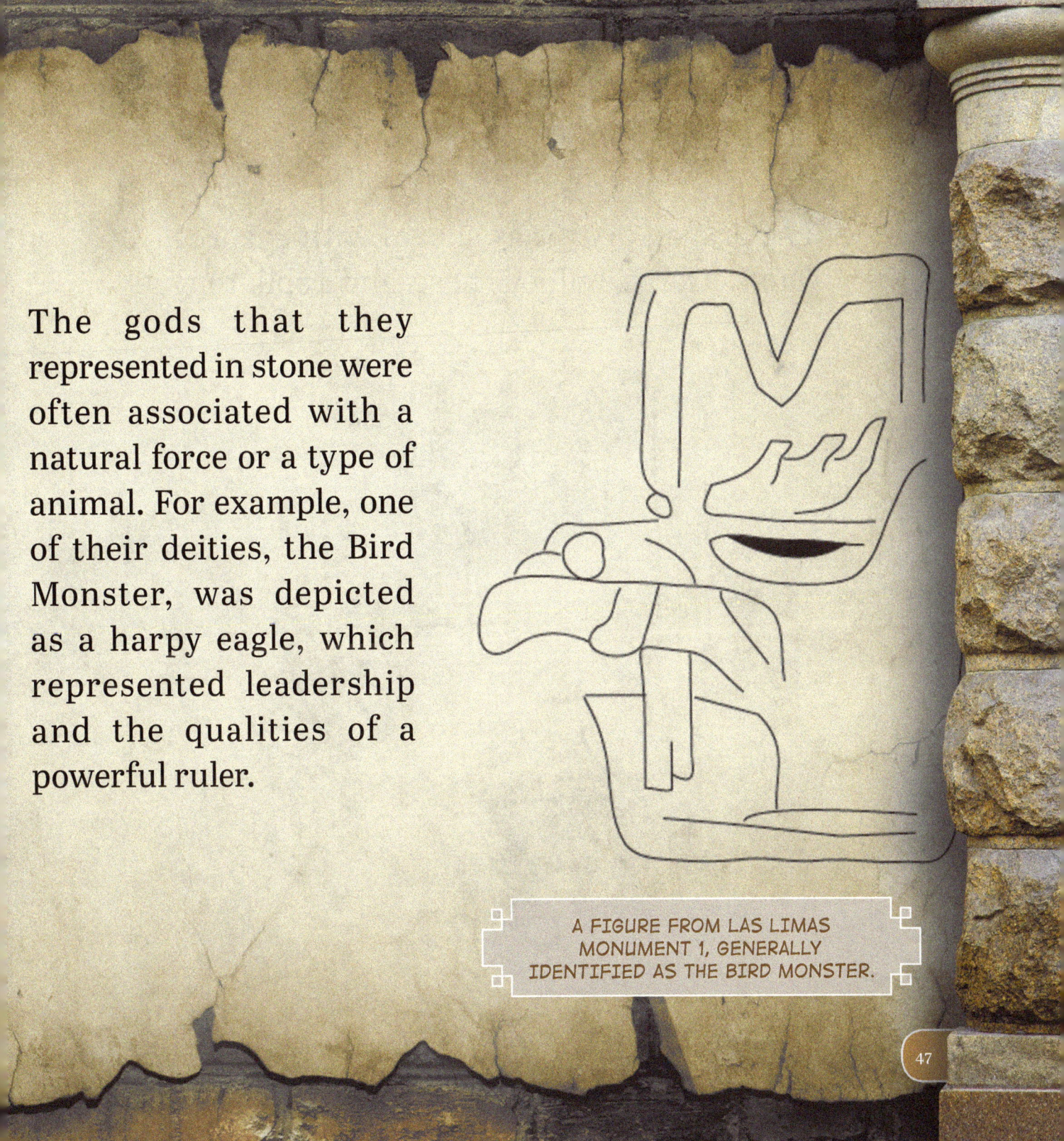

A FIGURE FROM LAS LIMAS MONUMENT 1, GENERALLY IDENTIFIED AS THE BIRD MONSTER.

The dragon deity was shown with eyebrows of flame, a large, bulbous nose, and a split tongue.

THE DRAGON DEITY

Maize was an important crop in their culture, so it's not surprising that they worshipped a Maize god.

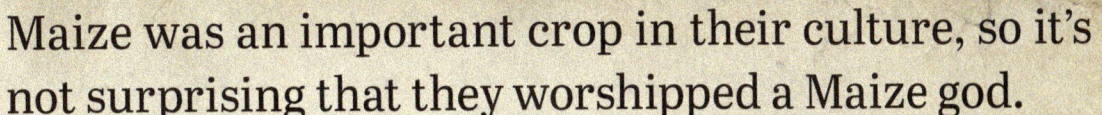

CUP WITH PROFILE HEAD OF THE MAIZE GOD

The Rain Spirit, also known as the Were-Jaguar, and the Fish Monster, also known as the Shark Monster, were also important deities.

OLMEC RAIN SPIRIT ALSO KNOWN AS THE WERE-JAGUAR

OLMEC SHARK-MONSTER DEPICTED ON THE INTERIOR BASE OF A CERAMIC PLATE FROM TLAPACOYA.

Archaeologists believe that the sites at La Venta and also at San Lorenzo were designed for the elite leaders and shamans, who used magic for spiritual and physical healing. More than likely there were a class of priests dedicated to presenting offerings to the gods in these two cities as well.

COLOSSAL OLMEC HEAD IN SAN LORENZO, TENOCHTITLAN

OLMEC "ALTAR OF THE CHILDREN" IN LA VENTA, VILLAHERMOSA, TABASCO, MEXICO

Olmec Expressions of Art

The Olmec people were master artists. They depicted the natural world by crafting art in jade as well as clay and basalt. They used greenstone, which is a word used by archaeologists to describe works of art created with minerals that are green. Many of the pieces of art that they created were depictions of the natural world that surrounded them. Other pieces showed creatures in the forms of humans.

SMALL BASALTIC OLMEC FIGURINE EXHIBITED IN FLORENCE, ITALY.

OLMEC JADE MASK

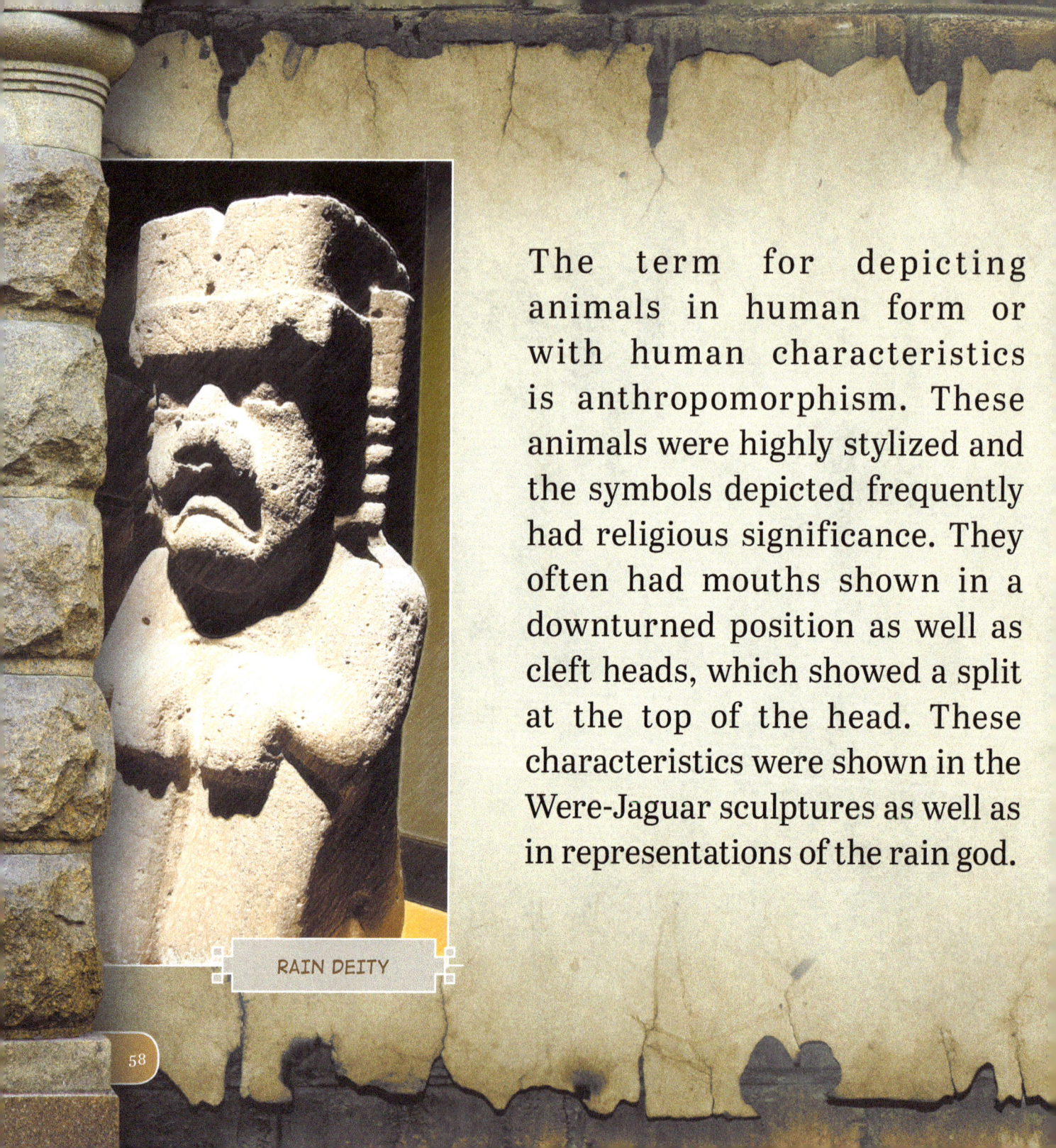

RAIN DEITY

The term for depicting animals in human form or with human characteristics is anthropomorphism. These animals were highly stylized and the symbols depicted frequently had religious significance. They often had mouths shown in a downturned position as well as cleft heads, which showed a split at the top of the head. These characteristics were shown in the Were-Jaguar sculptures as well as in representations of the rain god.

The style that the Olmecs used for their art is very distinctive and it is easy for archaeologists as well as art researchers to pick out artifacts that were crafted by the Olmec people.

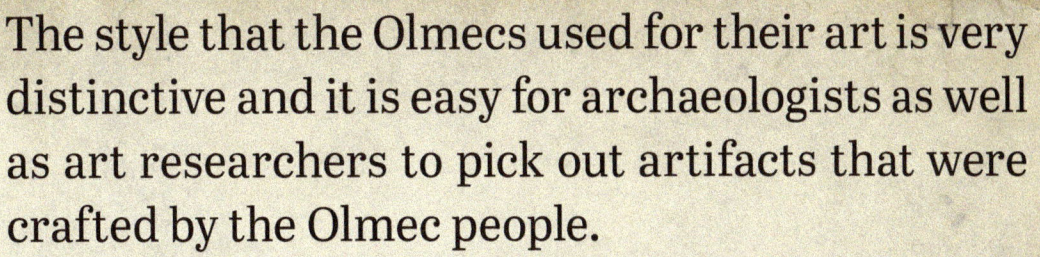

OLMEC JADE CEREMONIAL AXE

The Olmec people devoted a great deal of their time and energy to making art. The most distinctive of all their art are the enormous stone carved heads that are still in existence today. To date, seventeen of these heads have been excavated. These stone carvings, some as heavy as 20 tons, had been carved from large boulders of basalt, a type of volcanic rock.

COLOSSAL OLMEC STONE HEADS ON DISPLAY AT THE MUSEUM OF ANTHROPOLOGY IN THE HISTORIC CENTER OF XALAPA, VERACRUZ, MEXICO.

They date back to 900 BCE and are only found in the Olmec culture. They all show older men. The men have plump cheeks and flattened noses. They also have eyes that are slightly crossed. Even though they have these similarities, they are different men because they don't have the same exact faces and their headdresses are all unique as well.

GIANT OLMEC 40-TON HEAD DATING FROM 1000 BC IN PARQUE MUSEO DE LA VENTA, VILLAHERMOSA, CHIAPAS, MEXICO

These enormous boulders were transported to their ceremonial cities from the Tuxtlas mountain range. The incredibly heavy slabs of basalt were hauled over long distances, which means that it would have occupied time, hard labor, and an immense number of people. Just as archaeologists don't know fully how the giant stones were transported to create the pyramids of Egypt, the same is true in this case.

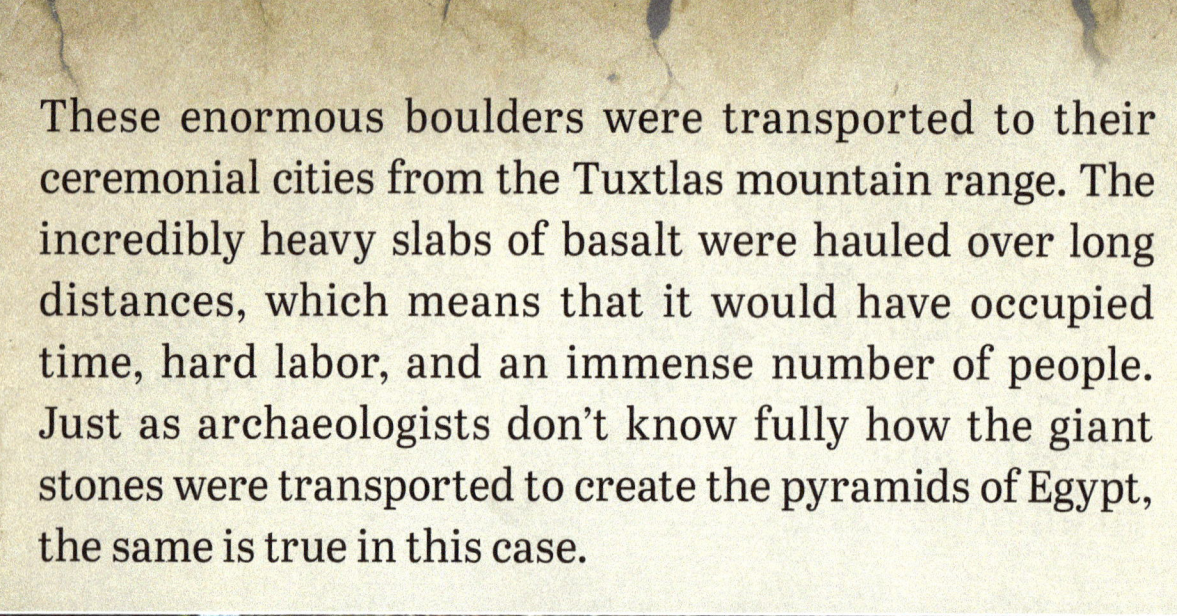

No one knows how the Olmec people transported these huge, heavy boulders to their ceremonial cities. Archaeologists are fairly certain that they are representations of the powerful Olmec leaders and that the sculptures might have been monuments to them after their deaths. The heads were displayed either in groups or in lines at the ceremonial cities.

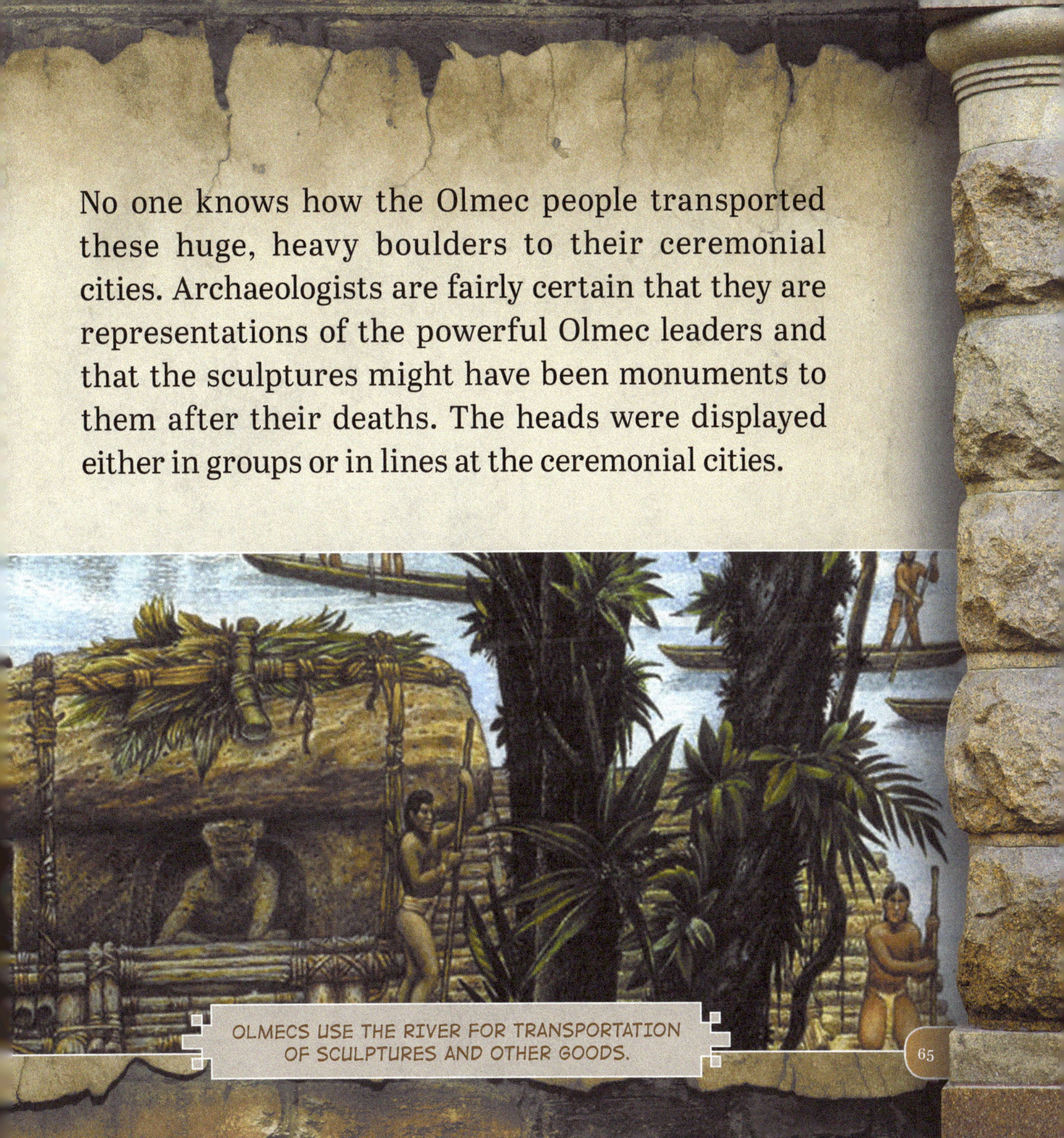

OLMECS USE THE RIVER FOR TRANSPORTATION OF SCULPTURES AND OTHER GOODS.

Around 350 BCE the Olmec civilization went into a steep decline. No one knows the exact reason this happened. However, researchers believe that changes in the environment caused the breakdown of their society. They believe that silting-up of the waterways meant that their source of water was cut off.

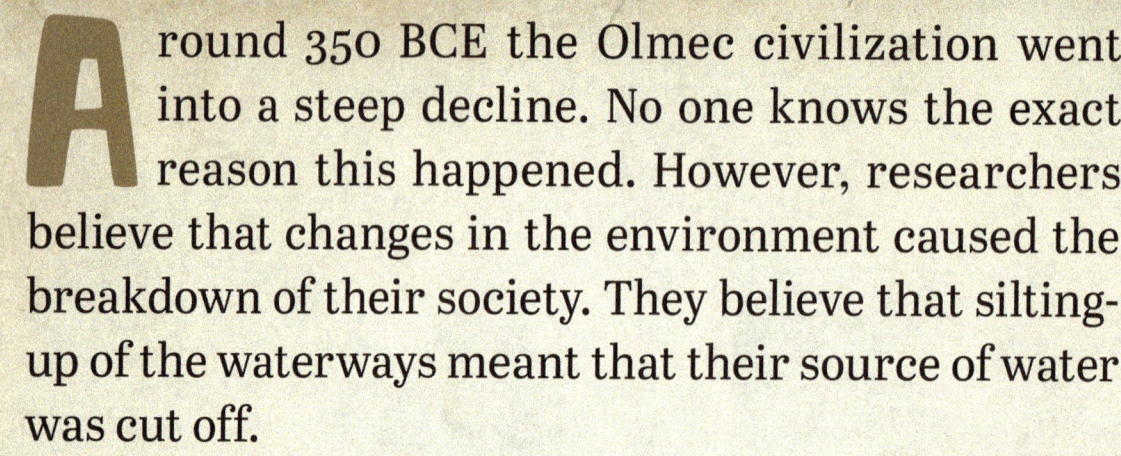

ARCHAEOLOGISTS BELIEVE THAT THE SILTING-UP OF WATERWAYS IS ONE OF THE MAJOR CAUSES FOR THE EVENTUAL DECLINE OF THE OLMEC CIVILIZATION.

Another theory states that volcanic eruptions in the area caused their land to be covered in deadly volcanic ash. This event would have been the impetus for them to leave.

VOLCANIC ERUPTIONS IN THE AREA CAUSED THEIR LAND TO BE COVERED IN DEADLY VOLCANIC ASH.

Summary

The Olmec civilization was a complex society that existed in the land we know as Mexico from 1600 BCE to 350 BCE. The ordinary citizens lived in small villages and subsisted from farming. There were two major cities, San Lorenzo and La Venta, where their rulers lived and their religious rituals took place. Archaeologists believe the Olmecs used their art to depict their rulers and to honor their deities. The gods they depicted had both male and female features. They also depicted animals with human forms and characteristics.

The most amazing of their many masterful artworks are the colossal human heads carved from basalt boulders. Researchers believe these heads, which still exist today, were created to honor their leaders after they died. No one knows how they carried these over 20-ton boulders to their cities. It's a mystery that may never be solved. In 350 BCE, this amazing civilization went into decline. Although the exact reason may never be known, it's believed that a huge environmental shift was the cause.

Awesome! Now that you've learned about the civilization of the Olmecs, you may want to read about Mayan civilization in the Baby Professor Book, *The History of the Mayan Empire - History Books for Kids | Children's History Books.*

Visit

www.speedypublishing.com

To view and download free content on your favorite subject and browse our catalog of new and exciting books for readers of all ages.

CPSIA information can be obtained
at www.ICGtesting.com
Printed in the USA
LVHW060148150322
713482LV00004B/29